THE ROMAN ARMY

PETER HODGE

Principal teacher of Classics, Lenzie Academy

LONGMAN

The Roman Army

The Roman army won Rome an Empire which by 100 AD stretched from the snowy mountains of Scotland to the hot sands of Syria and Egypt. Indeed, the story of Rome's rise to greatness is the story of how its army grew from a small band of noblemen into a large fighting force which conquered nations and spread Roman civilisation across the whole of western Europe and the Middle East. But that large fighting force was a very different kind of military organisation from a modern army.

The army formed after the foundation of Rome in 753 BC was probably made up of horsemen who were noblemen and foot soldiers who were ordinary citizens of Rome. About two hundred years later a different system came into force. The citizens were divided into classes according to wealth, and each class provided the men and equipment it could afford. The richest class were the 'knights' who provided their own horses and armour; the next richest provided their own armour and marched in the front ranks of the infantry; the poorer citizens who could not afford to buy equipment marched in the other ranks.

By the 3rd century BC the Roman army had become much more highly organised. It was now first and foremost a large force of heavily armed infantry troops, who fought shoulder to shoulder, a large oval shield in their left hand, and a spear or sword in their right. The infantry was supported now by only a small force of cavalry. The army also contained soldiers from countries which had become Roman allies. But the army was still made up of men who were recruited each year as part-time soldiers; there were no full-time professional soldiers. It was this kind of part-time army that fought against Hannibal and the Carthaginians in the war in North Africa.

In 106 BC, a new Roman general, Marius, set about reorganising the army. Marius made three important changes. (1) From now on any Roman citizen could serve as a full-time, paid soldier. (2) The army was divided into Legions made up of Roman citizens, and Auxiliary Forces (from the Latin **auxilium** meaning 'help') consisting of infantry and cavalry provided by Rome's allies. (3) Each legionary was now issued with the same dress and weapons: helmet, battle-dress, boots, a rectangular curved shield, two metal-tipped javelins, a pointed double-bladed sword and a dagger. In addition each man carried food rations, cooking pots, a spade, two stakes for building a camp, a hammer and a bag of nails and a military cloak which could be used as a blanket. Marius' army was a highly trained, well equipped and well organised professional army. This is the Roman army that this book is about.

How the army was organised

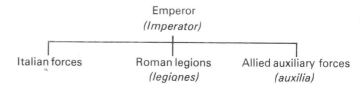

1: SOLDIERS OF THE EMPEROR

Organisation of the army

By the 1st century AD the Roman army was a highly organised and efficient fighting force. It consisted of:

Italian forces for guarding Rome and Italy and for the protection of the Emperor; they included the Imperial Guard, the City Cohorts, a small force of cavalry, police and fire-brigades, and the fleets which were stationed at Misenum near Naples on the west coast, and Ravenna on the east coast.

Legions made up of legionaries, who were Roman citizens mainly from Italy. There were 25–30 legions, each containing 5000–6000 men.

Allied auxiliary forces drawn from countries which were Roman provinces. They included cavalry and specialist infantry troops such as archers, slingers, and boatmen.

The supreme commander of the armed forces was the Emperor (**imperator**).

How the army was made up (rough figures)

30 legions of about 5000 men	150,000
Auxiliary infantry troops	140,000
Auxiliary cavalry	80,000
Irregular troops from allies	10,000
Italian forces	10,000
Total:	390,000

Statue of the Emperor Augustus dressed as commander-in-chief (*imperator*)

Italian forces: The Imperial Guard

The Emperor was protected by a force of specially picked men called the **Praetorian Guard.** To be a guardsman you had to be a Roman citizen from a good family and swear complete loyalty to the Emperor. The guards had special privileges, and better pay and conditions than the ordinary legionary. They served for 16 years.

Most of the time the guards were stationed in the Praetorian Barracks on the outskirts of Rome. They accompanied the Emperor, however, if he left Rome to command the army in the field.

The picture here shows a group of guardsmen in their uniform. Notice their crested helmets, their battle-dress and breastplates over the top of a tunic, their curved oblong shields, and the sword which one of them is carrying. On their feet they are wearing military sandals. In the back row you can also see a guardsman carrying a javelin, and the standard-bearer wearing a lionskin and holding the eagle standard or regimental colours.

A group of soldiers from the Praetorian Guard (from a relief)

The Legions

The Legions consisted of Roman citizens who signed on as full-time, paid professional soldiers. Each legion contained just over 5000 legionaries. The way in which a legion was divided up is shown in the diagram below.

Each legion was divided into 10 cohorts (**cohortes**) of about 500 men each.

Each cohort was made up of 6 centuries (**centuriae**).
Each century was made up of 80 men.
So there were 480 men in a cohort.
The first cohort in the legion, however, was a double cohort.

Each century was made up of 10 mess-tents (**contubernia**).
Each mess-tent had 8 men.
This explains why there were 80 men in a century, and not 100, as you might expect from the meaning of the word 'century' today.

How a legion was organised

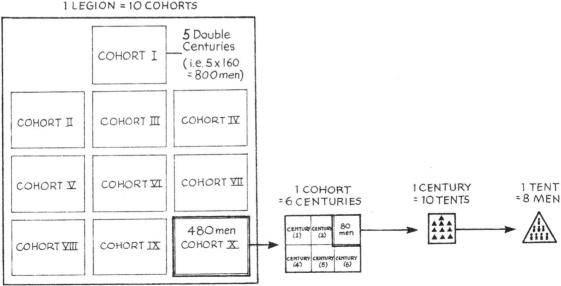

Far left:
Tiles found near Chester showing the emblem of the Legio XX Valeria.

Left:
A detailed close-up

There were probably 25 legions during Augustus' reign. Each legion had a *number* and a *title*. For example, the 4 legions originally sent to Britain were:

'The Emperor Augustus' Second Legion': LEGIO II AUGUSTA
'The Ninth Spanish Legion': LEGIO IX HISPANA
'The Fourteenth Combined Legion': LEGIO XIV GEMINA
'The Twentieth Valerian Legion': LEGIO XX VALERIA

(We can tell this from inscriptions on buildings, tombstones and tiles that have been found.)

Modern regiments in the British Army have similar titles: for example 'The King's Own Scottish Borderers', 'The Tenth Hussars', 'The Worcestershire and Sherwood Foresters'.

Each legion also had its own **emblem** and **standard**, just as regiments today have a mascot and colours. For example, the 1st battalion of the Worcestershire and Sherwood Foresters regiment has a ram as its mascot. On this page are two examples of Roman legionary emblems found in Britain. Can you say what the emblems are and to which legions they belonged?

Below: The emblem of the Legio II Augusta — a goat and a winged horse called 'Pegasus'

Eagles and standards

Each legion had its own standard in the form of an eagle (**aquila**) made of gold or silver. It was carried into battle by the Standard Bearer or 'Eagle-Bearer' (**aquilifer**).

The eagle was the symbol of Roman power and each legion was proud of its eagle. For this reason it was closely guarded by the First Cohort and its loss or capture by the enemy was considered a terrible disgrace. The legionaries would rather die fighting than surrender the eagle to the enemy. When the legion went into battle, the eagle led the charge and helped to rally the men. Some standard-bearers showed tremendous courage in leading the charge. Caesar in his description of the invasion of Britain in 54 BC tells us about the bravery of one *aquilifer*.

The Romans were hesitant because of the depth of the water when the eagle-bearer of the 10th legion, after praying to the gods that his action might bring them luck, cried: 'Jump down, comrades, unless you want to surrender the eagle to the enemy. I at least intend to do my duty to my country and my general.' With these words he jumped from the ship and advanced on the enemy with the eagle in his hands. When the other soldiers saw this, they urged each other not to allow such a disgrace to happen and also jumped while the men in the ships behind followed them.
Caesar *The Gallic War* 5.1

To be an *aquilifer* was a great honour and carried with it the rank of an officer. The post was often held by a veteran soldier nearing retirement.

A sculpture of an *aquilifer* of the Legio XIV Gemina found at Mainz in Germany (from a tombstone).
Notice the 'eagle' in his right hand and the decorations he is wearing on the front of his battle-dress—two torques and a set of medals (*phalerae*).

Besides the eagle, the legion also had several standards called **signa**. These had a hand emblem at the top. Each of these standards was carried by a standard bearer (**signifer**).

The picture on the left shows the tombstone of a *signifer* serving with the Ninth Legion in Britain. It was found at York and reads as follows:

In his right hand he is holding the standard with the hand emblem at the top and the medals won by his unit in its campaigns. In his left hand he is carrying a bag, probably the money-bag containing the soldiers' savings which the *signifer* was responsible for looking after.

L.DVCCIVS.	LUCIUS DUCCIUS RUFINUS
L.VOL.RVFI	SON OF LUCIUS OF THE VOLTINIA TRIBE
NVS.VIEN	FROM VIENNE
SIGN.LEG.VIIII	SIGNIFER OF THE NINTH LEGION
AN.XXIIX	AGED 28 YEARS
H.S.E.	HERE LIES BURIED

A signifer

Right: A group of infantry soldiers and two *signifers* (from a relief)

Senior officers

The commanding officer or general of the legion was the **Legate**. He was usually a Roman citizen who had already been a high-ranking government official, and he was directly responsible to the Emperor.

His second-in-command was the **Senior Tribune** who wore a broad stripe on his tunic to show that he was a member of the Senatorial class.

Below him was the **Camp Prefect**.

Below these were 5 junior staff officers, or **Military Tribunes**, who were from the Equestrian or 'Knights' class.

All these officers were attached to the staff at legionary headquarters. They were assisted by adjutants, orderlies and clerks. Unlike the ordinary soldier, they were excused the normal duties of daily camp life.

The emperor Trajan mounted on horseback (from a relief)

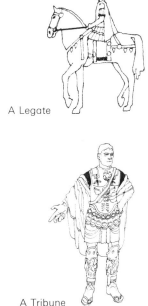

A Legate

A Tribune

Chain of command in a legion

Legate
(commanding officer)
|
Senior Tribune
(second-in-command)
|
Camp Prefect
|
Tribune
(Each legion had 5 tribunes
who were in charge of 10 cohorts)
|
Centurion
(In charge of 80 men)
|
Deputy centurion
Administrative and clerical staff,
engineers, doctors, priests
|
Legionary
|
Cooks, waggoners

Centurions

Of all the officers in a Roman legion the most important was the **Centurion**.

There were 60 centurions in each legion.

Each centurion commanded a century of 80 men.

Most centurions had won promotion the hard way from the ranks. They were responsible for the day-to-day command of the 80 men in their century, for leading their men into battle and for various administrative jobs in camp. They were also responsible for keeping discipline and for punishing soldiers who stepped out of line. And so each centurion carried a staff or swagger-stick made of tough vinewood, which became almost a badge of office.

The historian Tacitus, describing a mutiny that occurred in a legion serving in Germany, tells us that:

. . . a centurion named Lucilius was killed by his troops at the start of the mutiny. This man had earned their hatred because of the punishments he handed out to his men. They had nicknamed him 'Cedo alteram' (or 'Gimme another') because every time he broke his vine-stick on a soldier's back he called for another.

Tacitus *Annals* 1.23

There seem to have been different grades of centurion in the legion. The chief centurion of the whole legion was the **primus pilus**, or 'first spear'.

A Centurion

The tombstone of a centurion called Marcus Favonius Facilis was found at Colchester.

It shows Facilis dressed in his uniform – a pleated tunic with a breastplate on top and shoulder-pieces and a belt studded with the decorations that he had won. Over his left shoulder hangs part of his military cloak and round his neck is a scarf to prevent his neck from being chafed. His left hand rests on the hilt of his sword which hangs from a cross-belt on his left hip. In his right hand he carries his vine-stick. His legs are protected by metal greaves, or shin guards, while on his feet he wears military hob-nailed sandals.

The inscription underneath reads:

M FAVON M F POL FACI
LIS > LEG XX VERECVND
VS ET NOVICIVS LIB POSV
ERVNT H S E

And here is a translation of the inscription:

MARCUS FAVONIUS FACILIS, SON OF MARCUS OF THE POLLIA TRIBE,
CENTURION OF THE TWENTIETH LEGION,
VERECUNDUS AND NOVICIUS HIS FREEDMEN
SET UP THIS TOMB. HERE HE LIES BURIED.

The sign > shows he was a centurion.

It was probably the ambition of every legionary to become a centurion. If he proved himself as a soldier, he could expect to be promoted in time to the rank of Orderly Sergeant (or **tesserarius** as he was called, from the Latin word *tessera* meaning 'password'). He was the man who told the men the password at the beginning of each day.

From orderly sergeant the soldier might win promotion to the rank of *signifer* in his cohort. After that he could become a Deputy Centurion, called an **optio**. If he proved himself to be a good deputy centurion he might become a senior deputy (or, as the Romans said, **optio ad spem ordinis**, meaning 'deputy with hope of promotion').

The tombstone of an *optio* of the Twentieth Legion was found at Chester. His name was Caecilius Avitus and his home town was Emerita Augusta (modern Merida) in Spain. In his right hand he holds his staff, and from his right hip hangs a sword. In his left hand he is carrying a bag, with another bag or wallet on his belt. They probably contained money and documents belonging to the men in his cohort.

Here is a translation of the inscription on the tombstone:

TO THE SPIRITS OF THE DEPARTED
CAECILIUS AVITUS
FROM EMERITA AUGUSTA (IN SPAIN)
OPTIO OF THE TWENTIETH LEGION
SERVED 15 YEARS
LIVED 34 YEARS
LIES BURIED HERE

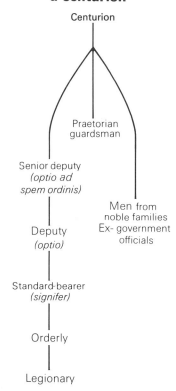

How to become a centurion

Centurion

Praetorian guardsman

Senior deputy
(optio ad spem ordinis)

Deputy
(optio)

Men from noble families
Ex- government officials

Standard-bearer
(signifer)

Orderly

Legionary

Legionaries

The backbone of the legion was the ordinary legionary or common soldier (**miles gregarius** meaning 'a soldier of the common herd'). By the 1st century AD the legionary was a well-equipped, highly trained, professional soldier. When he enlisted as a recruit, he signed on for 20 years with an annual pay of about 225 denarii (or 900 sesterces). But he did not receive all this in his hand. After deductions for food, clothing, equipment, and subscriptions to a burial fund, he was probably left with little more than half his pay.

When a man enlisted, it helped if he had a letter of introduction like this:

To Julius Domitius, legionary tribune
from Aurelius Archelaus, his orderly

Greetings. I have recommended my friend Theon to you before and I beg you once again to look on him as you do me. For he is the kind of man you like. . . . I beg you to let him have an introduction to you and he can tell you all about our business himself. Keep this letter in front of you, Sir, and imagine that I am addressing you in person. Goodbye. Papyrus *Oxyrhynchus* 1.32

Before being accepted for the army, each recruit had to have an interview (**probatio**) and a medical examination. He had to be a full Roman citizen or the son of a soldier, to be at least 5ft 8in tall, to have good eyesight, and to be in good physical shape. Slaves could not enlist in the army because they were not Roman citizens.

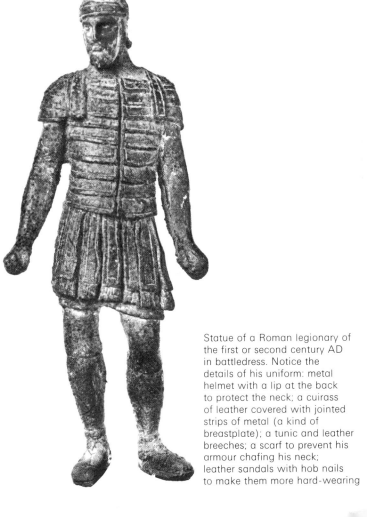

Statue of a Roman legionary of the first or second century AD in battledress. Notice the details of his uniform: metal helmet with a lip at the back to protect the neck; a cuirass of leather covered with jointed strips of metal (a kind of breastplate); a tunic and leather breeches; a scarf to prevent his armour chafing his neck; leather sandals with hob nails to make them more hard-wearing

Model of a
Roman
Legionary

If he passed his interview and medical, the recruit took the military oath of allegiance (**sacramentum**), in which he swore 'to perform with enthusiasm whatever the Emperor commands, never to desert, and not to shrink from death on behalf of the Roman state'. (Vegetius 2.5)

All legionaries wore the same uniform.

His weapons included a curved, rectangular shield (**scutum**) made of wood covered with hide. It had an iron boss in the centre for turning away enemy weapons. He carried this shield on his left arm. He was also issued with two throwing spears (**pilum**) with iron tips which were hinged to the shaft so that they would break off when they hit an enemy shield. In this way they could not be re-used by the enemy. He also carried a sword (**gladius**) and a dagger (**pugio**) for use in hand-to-hand fighting.

As well as all this, the legionary had to carry a great deal of equipment. This included a pack with 3 days' rations, cooking pots, an axe for felling trees, a sickle for cutting corn or clearing a path, a basket for shifting earth, a spade for digging ditches, a saw, a chain and a rope. He was also issued with a cloak which could be used as a blanket. With all this to carry, the legionary was rather like a pack animal. It was hardly surprising that he was given the nickname 'Marius' mule' (**mulus Marianus**)! (Marius was the name of the general who had re-organised the Roman army.)

Support services

The legions contained a vast number of other men besides the soldiers who served the army in the field. They included bakers, cooks, orderlies, armourers, carpenters, blacksmiths, waggoners and so on. There were also priests, doctors and musicians attached to the army, as we can see from the tombstones that have been found.

The army was supported on its overseas campaigns by a fleet and marines. When the Romans invaded Britain they needed a fleet to transport the legions, their equipment, horses and supplies across the English Channel.

Mosaic showing Roman transport ships

A Marine (relief from a tombstone)

Auxiliary forces: Cavalry

The Auxiliary Forces provided by Rome's allies consisted of cavalry and specialist infantry units.

The cavalry (**equites**) were organised into units called 'wings' of 500 and 1000 men, under the command of a cavalry officer or 'prefect'. Each wing was usually divided into 16 or 24 squadrons, which were commanded by 'decurions'.

The cavalryman was armed with a thrusting spear and a long sword (called a **spatha**). He wore a helmet, a coat of chain mail or scale armour with a tunic and breeches underneath, and carried a small round or oval shield (**clipeus**). He rode with his shield on his left arm and holding the reins in his left hand. In his right hand he carried his spear. He had a saddle and bridle but no stirrups.

At Gloucester there is the tombstone of an auxiliary cavalryman called Rufus Sita who was serving with the Sixth Cohort of Thracians. The Thracians came from Thrace in the north-east part of Greece. The inscription reads:

RUFUS SITA, CAVALRYMAN
SIXTH COHORT OF THRACIANS
AGED 40 YEARS
SERVED 22 YEARS
HIS HEIRS IN ACCORDANCE WITH HIS WILL
SAW TO THIS TOMB.
HERE HE LIES BURIED.

How the auxiliary cavalry was organised

Cavalry
(equites)

Prefect
in charge of an *ala* of 500/1000 men

Decurion
in charge of a squadron (16–24 squadrons each *ala*)

Cavalrymen   Archers   Slingers

Auxiliary forces: Infantry

The auxiliary infantry (**pedites**) were organised into cohorts of 500 or 1000 men and not into legions. Each cohort was commanded by a *Roman* officer — a tribune for a 1000-man cohort, and a prefect for a 500-man cohort.

An Auxiliary Infantryman (from a relief)

Each of the cohorts was divided into 6 or 10 centuries. A *Roman* centurion was in charge of each century. The rest of the soldiers in the auxiliary infantry were soldiers from Rome's different allies in the provinces of the Roman Empire.

There was always a danger that auxiliary forces might revolt or desert, so the Romans always put Roman officers in charge of auxiliary troops and also posted the auxiliary soldiers to units away from their own countries. This is why we find that most of the auxiliary troops serving in Britain came from other countries. When British men enlisted in the army, they were posted abroad to countries like Spain, Belgium, Thrace, and Syria. In this way they could not be so easily tempted to desert.

How the auxiliary infantry was organised

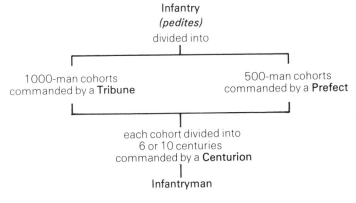

Infantry
(pedites)
divided into

1000-man cohorts commanded by a **Tribune**

500-man cohorts commanded by a **Prefect**

each cohort divided into 6 or 10 centuries commanded by a **Centurion**

Infantryman

An Archer

A Hamian
archer with
his bow
(from a
tombstone)

The auxiliary infantry were less heavily armed than the Roman legionaries and their equipment was different. They wore a helmet with a ring at the top, a tunic and breeches with a coat of chain mail or scale armour over the top sometimes, and carried a long sword instead of the legionary's short sword, and a round or oval shield instead of the Roman rectangular shield. Because they were lighter-armed than the legionary they were faster, but they also could be wounded more easily. They were often the first into battle and suffered heavy casualties.

Specialist troops

The auxiliary infantry also included specialist troops — archers from Syria, slingers (or **Balearici** as they were sometimes called, because they originally came from the Balearic Isles off the coast of Spain), men skilled in digging tunnels under enemy fortifications, and boatmen from the River Tigris in Iraq who acted as river pilots.

There were also units of auxiliary irregular troops (**numeri**) which were less well trained than other troops and fought using the weapons of the countries from which they came. They were less well organised than the legions and allied auxiliaries, and were commanded usually by their own tribal chieftains.

A lead sling shot ($4\frac{1}{2}$ cm long)

Organisation of the whole Roman army in the 1st century AD

Emperor
Commander-in-Chief of all Armed Forces

ITALIAN FORCES
Stationed in Rome and other parts of Italy

Imperial Guard
served for 16 years

Imperial Cavalry

City Cohorts

Police & fire brigade

Fleets at Misenum and Ravenna

TOTAL=approx. 10,000 Italian Forces

25–30 ROMAN LEGIONS (legiones)
consisting of freeborn full Roman citizens

Organisation of 1 Legion

A. INFANTRY (Pedites)

1 Legion=5,000–6,000 men

divided into

10 Cohorts
(1 Cohort=480 men)
i.e. 6 centuries

divided into

60 Centuries
(1 Century=80 men)
i.e. 10 mess tents

600 Mess Tents
(1 mess tent=8 men)

B. CAVALRY (equites)

120 cavalrymen in each legion
under 1 **Prefect of Horse**
Administrative Staff at HQ, Doctors,
Priests, Engineers, Bakers, Cooks,
Blacksmiths, Carpenters,
Waggoners, etc.

Chain of Command

OFFICERS

1 Legate (i/c Legion)

1 Senior Tribune
1 Camp Prefect
5 Military Tribunes

1 Eagle-Bearer (aquilifer)

60 Centurions
(1 centurion i/c century)
Deputy Centurions

Standard-Bearers (signiferi)
Tesserarii

MEN

Legionaries
● heavily armed
● highly trained
● served for 20 years
(+5 years as veterans)

TOTAL=approx. 150,000 Roman Legionaries

ALLIED AUXILIARY FORCES (auxilia)
provided by the provinces of the Roman Empire

Organisation of forces

A. INFANTRY (Pedites)

Organised in units of
EITHER

1,000-man Cohorts

each divided into

10 Centuries
(1 century=80 men)
(i.e. 10×8 men)

OR

500-man Cohorts

each divided into

6 Centuries
(1 century=80 men)
(i.e. 10×8 men)

B. CAVALRY (equites)

Organised in

Wings (alae)

each divided into

16–24 Squadrons

C. SPECIALIST TROOPS

Archers
Irregular troops (numeri)
Slingers

Chain of command

OFFICERS
EITHER

1 Tribune
(i/c 1,000 men)

10 Centurions
(1 centurion i/c 1 century)

OR

1 Prefect
(i/c 500 men)

6 Centurions
(1 centurion i/c 1 century)

MEN
Allied infantrymen
● less heavily armed
● less highly trained
● served for 25 years

OFFICERS
1 Prefect (i/c 1 ala)

16–24 Decurions
(1 Decurion i/c 1 squadron)

MEN
Allied cavalrymen

Total=approx. 140,000 Infantry+80,000 Cavalry+10,000 Irregular Troops
=approx. 230,000 Allied Troops

---

i/c=in charge

GRAND TOTAL FOR ARMED FORCES=approximately 390,000 men

QUESTIONS

1 Write down the three main divisions of the Roman army in the 1st century AD. (page 3) Who was the commander-in-chief?

2 Who protected the Emperor? (page 4)

3 Who served in the Legions? (page 5)

4 Look carefully at the diagram, then describe how a legion was organised. (page 5)

5 How do we know which legions served in Britain? Write down the name and number of the legion whose emblem was a goat. (page 6)

6 What was the legion's *aquila*? Who carried it into battle? To which legion did the man described by Julius Caesar belong? What did he do? (page 7)

7 What was L. Duccius Rufinus? How old was he when he died? (page 8)

8 Who commanded each legion? Write down the names of the officers below him. (page 9)

9 What kind of officer was M. Favonius Facilis? (page 11). How many were there in a legion?

10 Why was Lucilius nicknamed 'Gimme another'? (page 10)

11 What kind of officer was Caecilius Avitus? How old was he when he enlisted? (page 12)

12 How did the *tesserarius* get his name? (page 11)

13 What was a legionary? How much did he earn each year? How long did he sign on for? (page 13)

14 Why had Aurelius Archelaus written a letter to Julius Domitius? (page 13)

15 What tests did recruits to the legions have to pass before they were accepted? (page 14)

16 Why was the Roman legionary nick-named 'Marius' mule'? Describe his dress and equipment. (page 14)

17 What other men served in the legions? (page 15)

18 Who served in the Auxiliary Forces? What kinds of troops did the allies provide? (page 16)

19 What was Rufus Sita? To which unit did he belong? How old was he when he enlisted? (page 16)

20 Why were auxiliary troops posted away? (page 17) Write down the names of some countries which provided specialist troops. (page 18)

THINGS TO DO

1 Make a large wall-chart showing the different kinds of soldiers in the Roman army, based on the diagram on page 19. Try to draw each soldier's dress and weapons accurately, and beside each drawing write a brief description of what he did. You could make the chart as a group effort with some friends.

2 Draw a picture or make a model of a Roman legionary and an auxiliary infantryman. Label the different parts of their dress and weapons.

3 Imagine you are writing a letter of introduction for a friend who is wanting to join the Roman army. Write down why you think he should be accepted and try to persuade the recruiting officer to let him join the army. (You might find the actual letter on page 13 useful as a starting-point.)

2: LIFE IN CAMP

On arrival at his unit the recruit was given a course of basic training. This consisted of marching without arms, physical training, and weapon training.

The Roman writer Vegetius, writing towards the end of the 4th century AD, describes the training of recruits:

At the beginning of their training recruits must be taught the marching step. For nothing is so important on the march or in the field as all the men keeping their marching ranks. They will only learn to march quickly and in time with continuous practice. . . . And so in the summer months they must complete a march of 20 miles[1] in 5 hours at normal marching speed. When they march at the faster speed they must cover a distance of 24 miles in the same time.

Vegetius 1.9

Later on the recruit went on route marches in full battle-dress and carrying his arms and equipment, including rations.

The young soldier must be given frequent practice in carrying loads of up to 60 pounds[2] while marching at the normal speed, because on difficult campaigns they will have to carry their rations as well as their weapons. This is not difficult if they get enough practice.

Vegetius 1.19

[1] 20 Roman miles = 26 kilometres (18½ modern miles)
[2] 60 Roman pounds = 20 kilos

Left: Scene from the film 'Spartacus' showing Roman legions returning victorious from one of their campaigns

We cannot be sure how much the Roman soldier had to carry on the march. The modern soldier may carry up to about 30 kilos (66 pounds), so it is likely that the total load a legionary carried was between 30 and 40 kilos (60 to 80 pounds). It is not surprising that they were nicknamed 'Marius' mules'.

The Roman Army on the march, crossing a makeshift bridge of boats. Notice the standard-bearers in front, and the other ranks carrying their equipment on poles

Besides marching, the recruit underwent physical training which included running, jumping and swimming.

Weapon training was of two kinds — practice with dummy weapons, and mock fights using real weapons.

The early Romans made round wicker shields twice as heavy as those used in battle and gave recruits wooden sticks instead of swords, again double the normal weight. They practise with these at stakes morning and afternoon. A stake 6 feet high is fixed in the ground firmly. The recruit practises with his wicker shield and wooden stick against this, just as if he was fighting a real enemy. Sometimes he aims at the head or face, sometimes he threatens the thighs, and sometimes tries to strike the knees and legs. He gives ground, attacks and assaults the stake with all the skill and energy needed in real fighting against a real enemy.
Vegetius 1.11

After training with dummy weapons, the recruit took part in armed combat between pairs of soldiers, like the training fights of gladiators before they went into the arena. To prevent serious accidents the points of the weapons were tipped with leather buttons (like the points fitted to modern fencing weapons).

With all this training, it is not surprising that the Roman army was so efficient and disciplined. A Jewish writer called Josephus, who was captured by the Romans and watched them fight, remarked that in the Roman army 'their training was like a battle and their battles bloody exercises'.

Recruits practising dummy weapon fighting and undergoing physical training

Temporary camps

Having completed his basic training, the soldier was ready for active service with the legion. When not actually engaged in battle, the troops carried out regular route marches in full gear, and practised battle formations.

At the end of a day's march the legion pitched camp. When the army was on the move the troops lived under canvas. The Romans called it **sub pellibus**, meaning 'under skins', because their tents were made of animal hides.

Josephus describes the way the Romans built a camp:

Whenever they invade enemy country they never engage in battle until they have fortified a camp. . . . If the ground is uneven they level it. The camp is marked out in the form of a square. (The army takes a great number of workmen and tools with it just for building camps.) The interior is divided into rows of tents. The outside looks like a wall, with towers spaced out at regular intervals. Between the towers they position various artillery weapons for firing stones and arrows. There are 4 gates built into the rampart that surrounds the camp, one on each side.
Josephus *The Jewish War* III 72–75

Model of a Roman tent

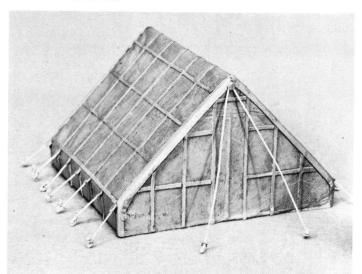

Layout of a temporary camp

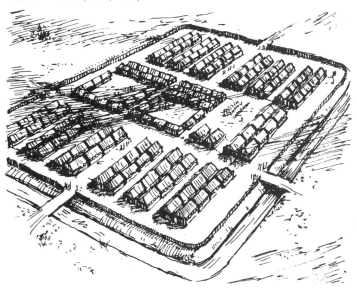

Vegetius describes how the camp was fortified:

There are 3 ways of fortifying a camp. If there is not too much immediate danger, turf is dug from the earth all round to form a kind of wall, 3 feet high, with a ditch in front from where the turf has been cut. In front of this an emergency ditch, 9 feet wide and 7 feet deep, is dug.

If the enemy forces are threatening to attack, however, it is worthwhile fortifying the outside of the camp with a full-scale ditch. . . . On top of this they raise a mound 4 feet high from the soil taken from the ditch, making the defences 13 feet high and 12 feet wide. On top of the mound they fix stakes of stout wood which the soldiers always carry with them. For building the trenches they find it useful to have pick-axes, shovels, baskets and other equipment always on hand.   Vegetius 1.24

Aerial view of Roman fort at Ardoch, Perthshire showing ditches and rampart

Soldiers cutting down trees and building a fortification of stakes

Soldiers building a stone or turf fortification.
Notice the different jobs being done and the tools being used, the dress of the soldiers who are working, and the set of equipment (helmet, shield and spear) at hand (at bottom right of the picture).

Every Roman camp and fort was laid out in the same way, whether it was a temporary camp with an earth ditch and wall like the one Vegetius describes, or a permanent fort built of stone.

Josephus describes what it was like inside a temporary camp.

The camp is conveniently divided into quarters by streets; the centre area contains the officers' quarters, with the general's headquarters right in the middle. It looks something like a city with its *forum*, the centre for craftsmen, and the offices where the tribunes and centurions settle disputes between the men.

The outer wall and buildings inside it are completed amazingly quickly, because of the number and skill of the workmen. If necessary a ditch 6 feet deep and 6 feet wide, is dug round the outside of the wall.
Josephus *The Jewish War* III 75–80

Look at the drawing of a Roman camp on page 24 and find the various parts mentioned by Josephus.

When the camp was fortified there was work to be done.

When the wall is built, the centuries go to their quarters in the tents, one by one, in a quiet and orderly way. All the camp duties are carried out in the same disciplined way — collecting wood, food and water when they are needed. The times for breakfast and dinner are organised so that they all take their meals together. The times for sleep, sentry duty and getting up are announced by trumpet-calls — in fact nothing is done without an order being given.

At daybreak the men report to the centurions. The centurions go together to salute the tribunes, and all the officers go to the general. He gives them the password, as usual, and the other orders that are to be passed on to the men.

Legionaries in camp

When it is time to break camp, the trumpet sounds. This is a sign for immediate activity. They take down the tents and pack everything ready for leaving. The trumpet sounds again for them to get ready. They quickly pile the baggage onto the mules and pack animals and stand at the ready, like runners at the starting-line waiting for the signal. Then they set fire to the camp to prevent it being of any use to the enemy since they can easily build another one for themselves. The trumpet sounds for a third time to warn those who are slow to hurry and so that no one is left out of his rank. Then the herald standing on the right of the general asks 3 times whether they are ready, and they reply 3 times: 'Aye, we're ready.'
Josephus *The Jewish War* III 80–102

Permanent forts

After a spell of duty in the field, the legion or cavalry unit would return to base. These bases were permanent forts that could hold a whole cavalry unit of 1000 men, or great fortresses like those at York, Lincoln, Chester or Corbridge (near Hadrian's Wall in Northumbria) which could accommodate a legion of between 5000 and 6000 men.

The permanent forts were built on the same plan as temporary camps but made of stone. They were larger and had much better quarters for the troops, as well as granaries, armouries, hospitals and bath houses.

The site of a fort was chosen with care. Forts were in key parts of the country, usually at the junction of the main roads and supply routes, or at river crossing places. They were often on high ground so as to give a good view of the surrounding countryside and be easy to defend against enemy attacks.

A good example of a fort like this is to be seen at **Housesteads** (on Hadrian's Wall), which provides us with a lot of evidence about the Roman Army in Britain. This fort could house a garrison of about 1000 auxiliaries. It was built looking towards Scotland on the edge of a line of crags with a drop of about 100 feet below it. To the south of the fort the ground slopes gently at first and then more steeply down to a river.

Round the fort stretched a wall with watch-towers at intervals. On each of the 4 sides was a gate-house with double gates and a guard room.

Above: Aerial view of Housesteads fort looking south.
Below: Reconstruction of the Roman fort at Housesteads with the North Wall at the top looking towards Scotland.

In the centre of the fort were the Headquarters (**principia**) where the general and his staff met to plan operations and discuss the day to day orders.

You entered the building through a paved courtyard at the far end of which was the **basilica**. You stepped into a long hall. At one end of the hall was a statue of the Emperor and at the other end was the raised platform and seat of the **tribunal**, where the general sat to address his officers and to deliver his judgement in cases where soldiers were being disciplined.

Opposite you as you entered the hall was the shrine or chapel (**sacellum**) where the legion's 'eagle' and the standards of the units were kept. Along the far side of the hall on either side of the chapel were the offices of the clerks and other administrative staff and a pay room where the soldiers received their pay.

Model of the Roman fort at Housesteads

1 Headquarters building
2 Commander's house
3 Hospital
4 Granaries
5 Workshops
6 Water tank
7 Latrines
8 Store

Hadrian's Wall

Scotland

North Gate

Hadrian's Wall

Barracks

West Gate

Via Decumana

5

4

3

1

Barracks

East Gate

Via Principalis

Via Praetoria

2

8

Barracks

Barracks

7 6

South Gate

England

The building also had a strong room where important documents, soldiers' pay and savings, and military decorations were deposited for safe keeping. There was also an armoury for storing weapons.

Left: Boss from a Legionary's shield, found in the River Tyne

Right: Bronze parade mask of a cavalryman found at Housesteads

Next to the headquarters was the general's house. It had several large rooms looking out onto a courtyard and had underfloor central heating (**hypocausta**).

At the back of the house was the general's private bath-house.

On the other side of the *principia* were the granaries, where the fort's grain supply was stored. The floor of the granary was supported by pillars which allowed air to circulate underneath to keep the corn dry.

Behind the headquarters was the fort hospital which contained several wards, store-rooms and a room where operations were probably performed. The only anaesthetic for operations was strong alcohol – a rather spine-chilling thought when you think of the number of amputations and operations to remove arrows which must have been carried out by the medical orderlies.

The granary at Housesteads

Roman surgical instruments

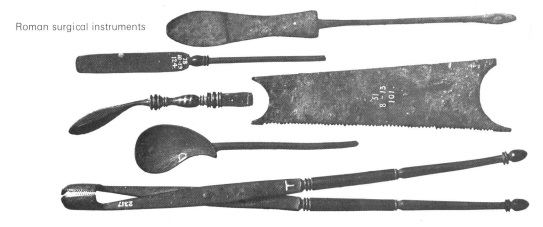

The rest of the fort was laid out in rows of barracks, workshops and store-rooms or stables. The barracks were built usually in pairs, facing each other across a narrow street. Each barrack block housed one century. At the end of each block were the centurions' quarters.

In addition to food supplies, each fort needed a supply of running water for drinking and for sanitation. In some forts this was provided by an aqueduct or pipes from a nearby stream. At Housesteads this was not possible so the Romans built several tanks for storing water. These had an overflow system which provided running water to flush out the latrines in the south-east corner of the fort. On either side was a water channel for washing out the sponges the Romans used instead of toilet paper. At one end was a wash-hand basin.

Most forts also had their own bath-house where the soldiers could relax and exchange stories as they sweated in the hot room or took a cold plunge. The bath-house was often situated outside the fort near to a river, as is the case at another fort on Hadran's Wall at Chesters where the remains of a fine bath-house can still be seen.

The latrines at Housesteads. The stone troughs were wash-basins.

Daily life in camp

When not out on exercises, route marches or campaigns, the soldiers were occupied in camp with drill and various duties: helping with the stores, cleaning and repairing equipment, and doing various chores. In addition each soldier was expected to take his turn at guard and sentry duty.

We know a little about what ordinary camp life was like from a record of the duty roster for a unit serving in Egypt when Domitian was emperor about 90 AD. Some people seem to have had an easy life — Gaius Domitius Celer ('Speedy') did nothing for eight days and then went on leave. Others were not so lucky. Marcus Arrius Niger ('the Black') was on barrack duties for a whole week, perhaps because he had not cleaned his equipment or had been sloppy on parade. Publius Clodius Secundus ('Lucky') had also been unlucky: he had had to clean his centurion's boots for three days running. The rest of the men were down for sentry duty, work in the armoury, or general duties like cleaning windows and moving sand, or cleaning the bath-house.

Barrack duties were one kind of punishment for minor offences. Others included having one's pay stopped for a time, being made to stand outside the general's office all day, or being flogged by the centurion in charge of your century.

But life in the army was not all work. At the end of a day when he came off duty, a soldier could relax with some of

Dice boxes and dice

his mates. Some would get together for a game like backgammon played with dice and counters on a board. Others would gamble with dice. And some would write a letter home to family or friends, or read their mail, like this letter which was found at Vindolanda near Hadrian's Wall.

I have sent you (some) pairs of socks, 2 pairs of sandals made in Sattia, and 2 pairs of underpants. Say hello to my friends and all your mess-mates. I pray that you and they may enjoy a long life and the best of luck.

Others might go into the nearby town or native settlement and spend the evening drinking in an inn. Some legionary fortresses, like the one at Caerleon in Wales, even had their own amphitheatre where the soldiers could watch wrestling, gladiator fights or horse-racing.

The night before a battle, however, was a time for checking your equipment — repairing a broken buckle, cleaning and sharpening your sword and dagger, and checking that all your equipment was ready for the morning. There would be no time for this sort of thing when the bugles blew the reveille.

The soldiers were excited, laying bets on who would win the most battle honours — a crown for outstanding gallantry, a medal, or arm-band. One or two wrote letters home to parents or sweethearts. And one or two slipped out to offer a prayer and make an offering to the god or goddess they believed would protect them.

Outside the barracks the sentries patrolled the walls, peering into the darkness beyond the fort. Everything was deathly still.

Legionaries 'off duty'. One is carrying his equipment and talking to a man carrying a standard.

QUESTIONS

1 The basic training of a recruit consisted of three things. What were they? (page 21)
2 What was the first thing a recruit learned, according to Vegetius? What were the normal and full marching speeds? (page 21)
3 What weight was the dress and equipment a legionary carried later on route marches? (page 21)
4 What two kinds of weapon training does Vegetius describe? Why were practice weapons tipped with leather buttons? (page 23)
5 What reason does Josephus give for the Roman army's strength and efficiency? (page 23)
6 What did it mean when a legion lived *sub pellibus*? What did a legion do at the end of each day when the army was on the move? (page 24)
7 How did the Romans build their camps? How did each century know when to move? (pages 24–27)
8 What stood in the middle of a Roman army camp? Where did the soldiers sleep? (pages 26, 29, 32)
9 How did the soldiers know when to go for their various duties and for meals? What kinds of duties did they have to do? (page 27)
10 In what ways were permanent forts (a) similar to and (b) different from temporary camps? (page 28)
11 Where did the Romans build permanent forts? Why is Housesteads fort so well positioned? (page 28)
12 What kind of fort was Housesteads? (page 28)
13 What would you see in the *basilica*? (page 29)
14 What other buildings stood near the Headquarters building in a Roman fort? (page 31)
15 At which Roman fort in Britain can you see an example of (a) granaries (b) latrines? (pages 31–32)
16 How do we know about what ordinary life in a Roman army camp was like? Describe briefly what kinds of things happened. (page 33)
17 How did Roman soldiers spend their leisure time? (pages 33–34)

THINGS TO DO

1 Draw a picture or make a model of a Roman camp or fort (pages 24, 28, 29). Label the different parts.
2 Imagine you are a recruit who has just finished his basic training. Write a letter to your parents or a friend telling them what life is like and what you have been doing.
3 Imagine you are in charge of building a Roman camp or fort. Write down instructions on how you want the soldiers to build the fort, including where the various buildings are to be sited, the sorts of defences it is to have and where the fort is to be situated.
4 Make a poster headed 'Roman Camps and Forts' and collect postcards, pictures from magazines and drawings. Find out if there is a Roman camp near your home, and try to visit it. Write a brief description of each photo or picture you put on your poster.

The Emperor Trajan ridi̶n̶g̶
at the head of a unit of
auxiliary cavalrymen
entering camp. In the
foreground soldiers are
using pick-axes to dig
ditches while others are
building a wall of turf.

3: EAGLES INTO BATTLE

The army on the march

It was dawn and the trumpets had already sounded the reveille. There had only been time for a mouthful or two of food. Already the men were lining up in their cohorts and the centurions took the roll-call. The trumpet sounded for the third time and they moved out. The legion was on the march.

Josephus describes the order in which the units of Vespasian's army advanced during the Roman campaign against the Jews in Palestine:

The auxiliary light-armed troops and archers were ordered ahead to meet enemy attacks and to explore the woods where an ambush might have been laid. Then came a column of heavy-armed Roman infantry and cavalry, followed by a detachment of 10 men from each century with their kit and equipment for marking out a camp site. After them came the engineers to clear, level and straighten the way for the army. Behind these Vespasian positioned his own equipment and that of his officers under a cavalry escort while he himself followed on horseback with a hand picked company of infantry and cavalry together with the lancers of the Imperial Guards as bodyguards.

Next came the cavalry units of the legions followed by various siege-engines and artillery drawn by mules. Another picked escort of foot-soldiers accompanied the legionary generals, prefects of the auxiliary cohorts and military tribunes.

Then came the standards with the eagle at the centre. The eagle goes in front of every legion because they look upon it as the king and bravest of birds, and a symbol of their imperial power. After the sacred standards came the trumpeters, and behind them the legionaries marching 6 abreast under the command as usual of a centurion.

Behind them came the servants leading the mules and pack animals with the soldiers' equipment. At the end of the column came an additional force of light and heavy infantry together with cavalry as a safety precaution to protect the rear.

Josephus *The Jewish War* III 6

Artillery and siege tactics

Roman artillery in the 1st century AD was of 2 main types: catapults (**catapultae**) which fired metal bolts and arrows, and stone-throwers (**ballistae**). Both were Greek inventions, which the Romans had copied, and were something like a mediaeval crossbow to look at. Instead of a bow, however, two wooden arms were inserted into rope-springs made of twisted animal sinew or hair. The arrow or stone was placed in a track in the middle and the draw-string between the arms was drawn back (like a bowstring) using a winch. The missile was fired by pulling a trigger which released the catch holding the draw-string.

By the end of the 1st century AD the Romans had developed a one-armed stone-thrower called an **onager**, so called because it had a kick like a mountain mule or 'wild ass'. This kind of stone-thrower was capable of hurling huge rocks at an enemy and causing great panic amongst the troops as well as being very destructive. Josephus mentions that the Romans used these 'wild asses' as well as other artillery against the Jews when they laid siege to the Jewish stronghold at Massada in 71–73 AD.

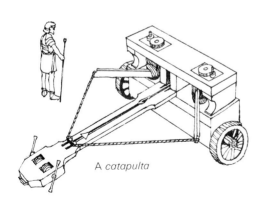

A *catapulta*

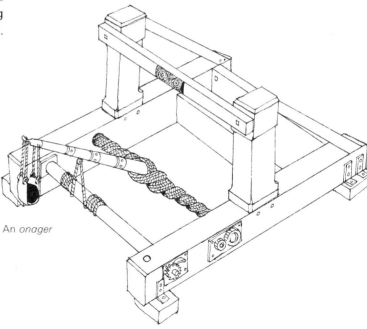

An *onager*

The troops attacking an enemy town needed some protection from the missiles hurled by the defenders, who would often drop heavy stones, shoot flaming arrows or pour boiling oil on the heads of the attackers. So, to protect themselves, the legionaries would be ordered to close ranks and form a **testudo**, or 'tortoise' formation. To do this they closed ranks to form a square or rectangle. Then the men on the outside held their shields so that they faced outwards while the men in the inside ranks held their shields above their heads. By interlocking their shields to form a solid wall around their ranks, the legionaries were protected against enemy missiles. It is said that the Romans sometimes tested the strength of a 'tortoise' formation by driving a chariot across the top of it.

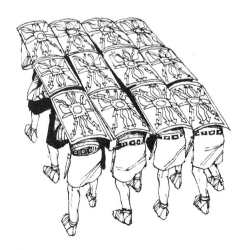

A relief showing tribesmen attacking a Roman camp with archers and a battering ram — one of the commonest siege weapons used by the Romans. As you can see, it was basically a pole made of timber (covered with hide to prevent the wood from splintering) with a metal knob at the end in the shape of a ram's head. The Romans also used a larger kind of battering ram suspended by ropes from a covered trolley, which could be wheeled up to the walls of an enemy town.

The siege of Marseilles

Julius Caesar describes how his soldiers besieged the town of Massilia (modern Marseilles) in 49–48 BC:

The people of Marseilles had been collecting for many weeks a large stock of arms and artillery for firing missiles, when Caesar's lieutenant Gaius Trebonius began to besiege the town and to bring up protective screens and siege towers. The enemy began by hurling beams 12 feet long with spikes on the end, which crashed through our protective wicker screens. Our men then built protective towers and a 'tortoise'* 60 feet long which went in front to level the ground and was covered, so as to protect the men from stones and burning torches hurled at them. . . .

The soldiers attacking the right-hand part of the town built a brick tower 30 feet square with walls 5 feet thick. They built the tower up as high as the first floor and covered the roof of it with bricks and clay and two pads of rags on top so that javelins from enemy ballistas could not break through the timbers or shots from catapults dislodge the brickwork. Then they gradually levered up the roof until the tower was 6 storeys high.

The next stage was the building of a gallery 60 feet long from the tower to the walls of the enemy town.

When the gallery was built, hides were laid over the bricks so that water could not be poured on to the bricks to split them up. The hides were covered with rags as a protection against fire and stones. When the gallery was completed, they placed rollers under it to bring it up alongside the walls.

The besieged inhabitants of Marseilles pushed huge rocks from the walls onto the gallery, but because of its strength they just rolled off. When they saw this they filled barrels with firewood and pitch, lit them and rolled them down from the walls onto the gallery. As they rolled down,

*The 'tortoise' Caesar mentions was a movable covered gallery.

Soldiers forming a tortoise to storm a fort

our men pushed them away with poles and pitchforks. Meanwhile under the gallery the soldiers used crowbars to pull apart the stones holding the foundations of the enemy wall, while other troops kept up a protective fire from the brick tower with javelins and ballistas. When several of the stones in the wall had been removed, part of the wall suddenly collapsed on top of it. When they saw this, the enemy rushed out of the gates unarmed and begged for a truce.

This was actually a trick to give the enemy time to recover, and the Romans were caught off guard.

A few days later when our men were relaxing during the lunch break, with their weapons laid down, the enemy suddenly burst out of the gates and set fire to our equipment. The siege wall, the protective screens, the 'tortoise', the tower and artillery weapons all went up in flames.

Caesar *The Civil War* II.1–15

The Romans hurriedly rebuilt their towers and a few days later forced the enemy finally to surrender.

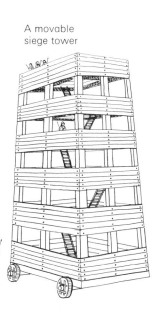

A movable siege tower

Building a siege tower to storm a town. Notice the ballista being manned by two soldiers (bottom right). There are two others mounted on the wall in the background. In the bottom left of the picture is a mobile *carroballista* mounted on a cart drawn by horses or mules.

Open battle

Besieging an enemy town was only one method of fighting. Often the Roman legions and allied auxiliaries fought pitched battles on open ground. The Roman historian Tacitus describes the battle fought against a force of about 30,000 British tribesmen under their leader Calgacus which took place at Mons Graupius (probably near the River Spey in Scotland) in 84 AD.

Before the battle began, Agricola addressed his troops, spurring them on to battle with words of encouragement and warning them about what would happen if they were defeated. The speech was greeted by a tremendous burst of enthusiasm from his troops. Tacitus then goes on to describe the battle which followed:

Agricola organised his troops with care. He arranged the auxiliary infantry numbering about 8000 men to form a strong centre, with 3000 cavalry positioned on the sides. The legions were drawn up in front of the rampart of their camp . . . so that the legions could come to the rescue if the auxiliaries were overwhelmed. The British forces were drawn up on higher ground. . . . The level ground between the two armies was the scene of noisy manoeuvring by British charioteers. . . . Agricola himself took up a position on foot in front of the legionary eagle.

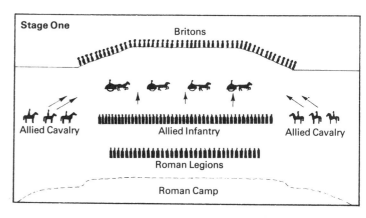

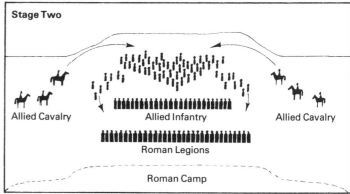

Diagram showing how the Romans defeated the Britons at the battle of Mons Graupius. In the first stage Agricola ordered the allied infantry to advance. Then, when the British infantry attacked, and tried to surround them, the allied cavalry were ordered to ride round behind and attack them from the rear.

The battle began with an exchange of missiles. . . . At last Agricola ordered 6 allied cohorts to close ranks and fight it out at sword-point. These veteran soldiers were very experienced at sword fighting, while the Britons were out of their depth with their small shields and large unwieldy swords which had no sharp point and were quite unsuitable for hand-to-hand fighting. The soldiers rained blow after blow on the Britons, striking them with the bosses of their shields and stabbing them in the face. Having cut down those who had been stationed on level ground, they advanced up the hill. . . . Meanwhile, the cavalry squadrons had routed the enemy chariots and now joined in the infantry battle. After a terrifying first charge, they were brought to a halt by a solid line of enemy.

The Britons then tried to surround the Romans, and began to descend and surround the rear, but Agricola ordered his cavalry to ride round and attack them from the rear. The Britons were cut to pieces.

The open plain now revealed a grim and awe-inspiring sight. . . . Equipment, bodies and mangled limbs littered the blood-stained earth. . . . The pursuit of the enemy went on until night fell and the soldiers were tired of the butchery. Some 10,000 enemy troops lay dead, while on our side we lost 360 men.

Tacitus *Agricola* 35–38

A legionary receiving first aid from a medical orderly while an auxiliary has a wound dressed.

Triumphal procession

When a victorious general and his army returned to Rome, they were usually given a triumphal procession. The general rode at the head of his army at the front of the procession, followed by his troops and prisoners who had been captured and brought to Rome as slaves. The crowds lining the streets cheered wildly, waving their arms and throwing garlands of flowers in their path. Sometimes the Roman Senate voted for a triumphal arch or statue to be put up in honour of the victory.

Scene from a triumphal procession showing the Romans taking the treasures from the temple in Jerusalem (from the Arch of Titus in Rome)

QUESTIONS

1 Read Josephus' description of the order in which the units of Vespasian's army marched (page 37). Write down the order: for example, (1) In front were allied light-armed infantry and archers; (2) Roman heavy-armed infantry and cavalry; and so on.

2 What two main types of artillery did the Romans use in the 1st century AD? From whom did the Romans copy? What did they fire? (page 38)

3 What was an *onager*? How did it get its name and what did it fire? (page 38)

4 Read Caesar's description of the siege of Marseilles. (pages 40–41)

   a What had the people of Marseilles done before the siege?

   b How did they try to beat off the Roman attackers?

   c What tactics did the Roman commander Trebonius use first of all? What was a 'tortoise'? (page 39)

   d What did the soldiers on the right part of the Roman forces build? How was it protected?

   e What did the defenders do?

   f How did the Romans approach the walls next? What were they trying to do?

   g What happened then? What did the enemy do?

   h After the truce what did the enemy do next?

   i What happened in the end?

5 Read the description by Tacitus of the Battle of Mons Graupius. (pages 42–43)

   a Where were the British forces drawn up? Why?

   b What did Agricola do before the battle? Why?

   c Where did Agricola arrange (i) the allied infantry? (ii) the Roman legionaries? (iii) the cavalry?

   d How did the battle begin?

   e What did Agricola do next? What happened?

   f What did the Britons do then?

   g What did Agricola do to prevent the Britons?

   h What was the outcome of the battle?

   i Why do you think Tacitus might be exaggerating?

6 What happened when a victorious general returned to Rome? (page 44)

THINGS TO DO

1 Make a frieze showing a Roman army on the march based on the description on page 37. Label the different troops.

2 Draw pictures or make models of Roman artillery and siege equipment from the pictures on pages 38–41. Write a few lines about the pictures you have drawn.

3 Imagine you are *either* a Roman general besieging an enemy town *or* one of the besieged inhabitants. Describe what you see and what you do.

4 Draw or paint a picture of a Roman siege like the one described by Julius Caesar.

5 Imagine you are a news reporter at the scene of the Battle of Mons Graupius. Write a report for your newspaper and draw a picture to illustrate it.

4: OLD SOLDIERS NEVER DIE . . .

Discharge and diplomas

After 20 years' active service with the legions, the legionary was transferred to a cohort of veteran soldiers (**veterani**), where he served for the last 5 years. (Auxiliaries served for 25 years altogether.)

Some soldiers were invalided out of the army before their time was up, but most completed their service, which was marked by an official discharge certificate (called a **diploma**). It was a bronze tablet which contained a copy of the soldier's service record; the original record was sent to Rome.

Several of these *diplomas* have been found in Britain, like the one shown in the picture here, which was found at Chesters fort on Hadrian's Wall. This one was given to an auxiliary soldier on completion of his 25 years' service. In return for his loyal service, it granted him Roman citizenship and made his wife legal. (Roman soldiers below the rank of centurion were not allowed to marry while serving in the army. However, many soldiers did marry and the Roman government included a section in a soldier's diploma which legalised such marriages and granted citizenship to any children born to Roman legionaries.)

A soldier also received a present of money as a reward for service, just as soldiers do on retirement today. A legionary during the 1st century AD received 3000 denarii, which was the equivalent of more than 10 years' pay, on discharge; soldiers in the Praetorian Guard received 5000 denarii at the end of their 16 years' service.

Part of a bronze *diploma* found at Chesters fort

Colonies . . .

Sometimes soldiers were given land instead of money, and settled in a colony (**colonia**) for veteran soldiers. Here they could settle down with their wives and children and cultivate a plot of ground in their retirement.

There were a number of these *coloniae* in Italy itself and scattered throughout the Roman provinces, including four in Britain at York, Lincoln, Colchester and Gloucester. There were also several in North Africa.

Some ex-soldiers returned to their own country, but many stayed on in the provinces on the very edge of the Roman empire, passing the twilight of their lives in the land that had been their home for many years.

. . . and tombstones

And, when they died, their families put up tombstones in their memory, many of which can still be seen to this day. These monuments to old-timers and the tombstones of those who died on active service provide us with a wealth of information about the way the Roman army lived . . . and died.

Timgad – a *colonia* for army veterans in Algeria

SOME IMPORTANT DATES (All dates are AD) (c = about)

9	Varus and 3 legions ambushed in Germany and massacred.
14	Revolts of Roman armies in Pannonia (Hungary) and Germany. Campaigns by Germanicus to avenge the massacre of Varus' army.
43	Second invasion of Britain by army under Emperor Claudius.
56–58	Corbulo's campaigns against the Parthians in Syria.
60	Revolt of Queen Boudicca in Britain and sack of Colchester, London and St. Albans. Paulinus puts the rebellion down. Revolt in Gaul.
68–69	Civil War: the Year of the Four Emperors (Galba, Otho, Vitellius and Vespasian). Revolts in Germany and Judea. Vespasian's campaign in Palestine.
71	Sack of Jerusalem by Titus.
71–73	Siege by Roman army of Jewish stronghold at Massada.
74–78	Petilius Cerialis' campaign in Britain.
78–84	Agricola's campaigns in Britain.
81–96	Emperor Domitian's reign: campaigns against Germans and Dacians.
98–117	Emperor Trajan's reign: campaigns against Dacians, Parthians and Jews.
c 122–130	Hadrian's Wall built in Britain from Solway Firth to the River Tyne.
c 139–142	Antonine Wall built by Lollius Urbicus from Firth of Clyde to Firth of Forth.
c 180–200	Frontier defences overrun: Emperor Septimus Severus rebuilds Hadrian's Wall.
287–297	Carausius and Alexander rule an independent empire in Britain.
407	Roman legions finally withdrawn from Britain.

7604